T0007487

A QUEEN IN BUCKS COUNTY

KAY GABRIEL

A QUEEN IN BUCKS COUNTY

NIGHTBOAT BOOKS

NEW YORK

ISBN: 978-1-643-62149-4

COVER ART: DAVID WOJNAROWICZ

UNTITLED FROM SEX SERIES (FOR MARION SCEMAMA) (HOUSE), 1988-89

GELATIN SILVER PRINT

COPYRIGHT ESTATE OF DAVID WOJNAROWICZ

COURTESY OF THE ESTATE OF DAVID WOJNAROWICZ AND P·P·O·W, NEW YORK

DESIGN AND TYPESETTING BY KIT SCHLUTER

TYPESET IN SORTS MILL GOUDY AND BERTHOLD AKZIDENZ GROTESK

CATALOGING-IN-PUBLICATION DATA IS AVAILABLE FROM THE LIBRARY OF CONGRESS

NIGHTBOAT BOOKS

NEW YORK

WWW.NIGHTBOAT.ORG

a queen in Bucks County
pulls on her glove to show her gold ring
tomorrow, tomorrow the wedding will begin

—LOUIS ZUKOFSKY, "A"-12

"In these rooms of sleep and of dream," she continued
in another of her letters which will become famous
after history has gone to sleep, "we will walk around,
brushing by each other, touching each other
without actually touching...."

—KATHY ACKER, *PUSSY, KING OF THE PIRATES*

CONTENTS

SIP HOLE

Dear Kay—

Men buy me things: uppers, cocktails, cab rides, or something more impressive. Who do I impress? A cheat, a villain and amateur coquette, I'm writing in the shadow of a Wawa, a pair of withering cities, their gutted suburban corridor. It isn't nice and there's nothing coy about it—except me, your mercenary of the 'burbs, your sip hole, your nipple aficionado.

Have I made you blush? I'm writing you perpetually in transit, shuffling somewhere, en plein air, a lollipop on SEPTA. I know what I look like, and what I'd like to: a pantsed River Phoenix? Enough to tease in good lighting, but just at present my audience is the bridge signing TRENTON MAKES—THE WORLD TAKES into a sullen Jersey. Presenting here my reeking autobiography, nobody around to take a bite. Would you?

Well, what do men buy you? I want one of these extravagant types to pay my rent. I want another to show up regularly with a carful of groceries, right at the end of the month when it really matters. I want a third to nurse my immaculate asshole with the kind of attention you lavish on a gift.

Dear Kay. These letters will be famous after history has gone to sleep. Till then I'll dazzle with my nipples on the inside of a shirt, fulfilling to the genre what Liza and the Pet Shop Boys did to "Losing My Mind"—elaborate, sustain, convoke a synthed-up neurosis ballad, not going left, not going right.

Now home, to push into a vacant 5 AM, and ruin every bit,

Turner

GRACE ZABRISKIE, Stephen,

sounds like jackoff if you do it right
athleticky, white and striped

a rumour glyphed in
cloth out of my hole:
"shut up"

Wrong
life cannot be lived
rightly, then there's the Pines

> Dopamine, ketamine, John Cazale
> Delict, persona, Howard Ashman
> Doppelbanger, tea service, Grace Zabriskie
> Diaresis, kohlrabi, Viktor Shklovsky
> De-lovely, tweaking, Donna Summer

In a park thick
enough to hang
a beard on

the hunk masseur pummels your bf's
ass like a doping cyclist
on the Tour! *quel* uphill climb

and the rain has commenced its
delicate lament over the orchards,
talented, having a great time

Once I looked out my apt. window
into the shaft to watch a V
of pelvis and an H of abs

a then-boyfriend jerked
me off with commas!

This bitch inside
with puppies yelps
when you prod her

the jockstrap advances,
a scratch-and-sniff of inspired method
a wail your boyfriend compares

to the abrasive giggle (mine),
a seam of buttock, or
an interview on live TV

I always wanted to feel better,
"This very talented upbeat
having a great time lady"

Caller, you're on air,
Turner.

SHUT YOUR MOUTH

Turner's voice goes up like a bark:
Another boy's coaxing his
sphincter, a dog
and his muzzle. On the fourth
finger he puts down his phone.

Five, and some suction.
It's not his fault he's short,
bent double like rammed in the nuts.
Turner arches up to, uh—
Ryan's?—forceps. Forearm.

Ryan's! He wants to turn around:
I know your name! But his orgasm
rips out of him, an acrylic nail caught
off a finger and torn. He noses
the Star Wars bedspread

Eases into a sopping Mark Hamill.
"Pull out, okay?" And he does, quiet,
complaisant. What does my
asshole feel like—silky and vacant?
The wrist exits and a curtain drops too.

Dog's off his leash. Ryan sinks
onto Darth Vader's mask. Turner's high,
so Ryan looks like a shoulder.
He shakes the poppers, *shut your mouth*.
The shoulder slips in & out of focus.

I DO MY BEST TO CHEAT

Dear Connie—

The leisure you need to have sex, well, the leisure you need
to write. It's leisure and everyone should have it; when every-
body does, it won't be leisure anymore, but something else,
like and also totally unlike a bed to sleep in.

Which is what I think I mean when we say writing should be
for everyone—but I don't speak for anybody, I'm not the first
to ask this question, neither the most nor the least leisured.
It's not a game and nobody racks up points, though I've got a
bag of someone else's stars. Time passes, not metaphysically;
I'm clocking in and out, I sleep on the ride home, I do my best
to cheat.

Skipping work is a tonic until you get busted for "time theft"
by those who stole it from you first. I steal from train con-
glomerates, but who'd convict me? A conductor? One walks
by with tattoos, surely a friend in the wrong uniform. But
actually he busts me over the clipped ticket, he doesn't buy
the Bambi act. You can't trust a guy for his ink—a fantasy,
Romantic as they go. Someday the pussy brigands will board
the train and shake down the guards for ticket stubs and pet-
ty cash. They'll ride each other through the cars, rip every
velcro strap, snap every button on every coat and liberate
yuppies of their iPhones.

I've never fucked in the bathrooms of regional rail. I've never
come hands-free. I'm in love with the future tense only, and
keep it on a high shelf or hanging from my rearview mirror. I
swear it'll take down the highway too, and whatever's left will
be for the rest of us.

Connie if it gets any colder my nipples'll get hard enough to slash through the front of my shirt. Men stare and run back to their wives. Maybe I'll write a novel and call it *The Daddies*, though this isn't strictly my type, whose appetites range too widely. For a while I borrowed my everything from Jacqueline Susann's *Valley of the Dolls*, milking its sometime mass appeal and limited imagination for a millennium of camp—back when I took benzos to fall asleep every night and watered down the 'burbs in a teacup of rye, a combo deal to stop your heart. When I go I'll go in the bath, I'll flood infrastructure with gory suds.

In Susann's masterpiece of entertainment industry blues Anne Wells skids into the city out of a New England blizzard, her features ripe to score a millionaire, and then she does. A wife's wife with barbiturates on tap, she doesn't want them much till they skid back out of her Romantic grasp. Can I wrestle something more than Deco interiors out of this document? Sexually conservative, it's obsessed with fags and dykes, Radcliffe girls ripping up their flowerbeds by the root, the life and death of vaudeville, getting your man to propose and lick you clean. As talentless stunner Jennifer North, Sharon Tate in the movie lilts *all I know how to do is take off my clothes*, and that feels about as right as pressure on the velveteen rope of a prostate.

Jennifer's the hapless con with good cheekbones who lies about her schoolgirl lesbian past and can't get a man to see past her top shelf. She goes out in a pop of melodrama, so I can't help feeling identified. Who's the Neely among us— the plain, dynamic self-saboteur with the good voice? Who's Anne? One of us who'll spill from grace onto an investment trampoline. I'll call that girl Money; I'll whisper her surly name over the phone.

Back to Sharon and what she knows how to do. The dads take them off for me, I think in profile I'm probably pretty cute though I don't know what they see when they look at me—someone slight and accommodating. Men buy me things. In a parallel life it's chasers, and in both the casting director picks out an antagonist of wives, a wife herself. Do I mind it? I think I mind it.

That's not quite right, I want to interrupt myself. Have you ever hosted a jock? He purrs like it's his first time, though there he's been on the apps and has the nudes to prove it. He's had a beer and then another, and then he offers you a bump, and by the time the drip hits—singeing, crappy and free—he's doing laps around you as if about to score the latest in a line of trophies. I picked up one like that from the neighborhood, actually it wasn't such a bad time. Knotted somehow between a high and a comedown I looked out my window at the illuminated fronts of loan shops and fast-food joints while he stretched my hole loose and swept past my dick like it wasn't there. Stuck on the soundstage for *Little Shop of Horrors*, a Lower East Side with a low and busted ceiling for a sky, did I match him grunt for plaintive grunt? Sure, but he smelt like every good thing.

He's a snowdrop in winter, liable to tear. Rip him up by the root and drop him in his own mulch. A blushing kid with a priapic corsage, he wants to be trundled into the vacuous thing that keeps him wet and warm. A low-hung slut, he wants to feel like the captain of his own highway, and peaceably oversee the flood that swings him into a ditch. Actually he offers to flip. The reader will suspect by now that I don't, like I suspect this champ of track-and-field has sprinted over to exercise his pelvic floor around a couple fingers and some black latex. Athleisurely in luck, the virgin blushes, the flower crumples, the runner cramps and the beveled road swamps away. At a nudge every gruff top rolls over to expose his belly and lift his hole around a pumping pair of hands. I pumped him into a flowerbed. I pumped him into a ditch, and now I'm telling you.

Is it leisure if I mind it? Turns out I didn't, not just for the compliment. *Your mouth feels like pussy,* he said, I ripped it out of him. Cradled between a hand in his ass, a hand on his cock and these prodigy lips, what else could he accuse? I feel like every good thing, I guess it does. *My mother was a vacuum cleaner* I like to joke, or *I'll put that one on my Yelp page.* Confused, he guided me back to his cock. I cradled, pumped and pushed and then he spouted like a broken water main. Goodbye high school. Goodbye homerun crush.

Epistoslut's on the scene. I used to stack the crud of this world in grids and lists. Now I put it in sentences, and interrupt them with a knife. I don't know that one is better except as it molds around the workday, I smuggle it home in a breast, it pays its way all dozen miles. What's it like, over there where they have highways?

Somewhere en route,
Turner

BREAD

Stephen—

You know when you feel like someone's idea of a good time.
All you have to do is open your mouth.

To make a particularly flavorful dough I prepare first a liq-
uidy sponge gasping with yeast, which I scatter with a blan-
ket of flour, salt, and more yeast to leave overnight. When I
come back in the morning the sponge has bubbled through
its blanket like water through peat, and a rich sour aroma has
started to bloom. "Let's go to the back room," Turner suggest-
ed. "I wanna suck some cock."

You can leave the sponge for a day or more in the fridge to
acquire flavor. When it's finally removed the carbon dioxide
produced by the anaerobic respiration of the yeast will have
punctured up the flour blanket with moist gouges of fetid
air, which is what you want. "What are you here for," Turner
asked Mike. He tilted his chin up like he'd won a bet. "Trying
to get my cock sucked."

Sometimes the bubbles rush out of the dough like a shaken
seltzer bottle when you smack it onto a counter. *Pure lugzhury*
Bernadette Peters in her commercial for Kleenex Classique
"softer and thicker" tissue *I can just throw away.* Before anal
Turner routinely inserted one, then two lubed fingers, around
which he would then clench and unclench his PC muscle,
making his cheeks gather attentively around the squeezed
lemon rind of his hole; then lift the fingers methodically to
his mouth, suck, suck. Each one, clean to look at, emitted a
whiff of sour particulars.

Mike's cock was wet. His chest and beard were wet like dim sweaty lights. Going downstairs to the party Turner and Cam smelled not sex but a basementy mildew, then beer and disco. To knead a stiff, medium-wet dough I scatter flour on a clean scrubbed counter, then punch the dough into a fragrant blob until it adheres more to itself than to my hands. What's the right verb for the ache of anticipation Turner felt pulling down Mike's jockstrap below his knees? Reader, I thrummed towards his furred thighs. I ringed him like a sleeve.

Often I begin the kneading process agitated like I've had a cup of coffee and continue till I discover some satisfaction. It's difficult to overmix a dough by hand. Did he like to get fingered? Turner didn't know but when he tongued the outside he picked up Mike's smell, a bee furred in pollen.

By the time I've shaped a loaf and prepared it to rise a second time the smell of the dough is milder, but if refrigerated the fermenting yeast will produce acetic rather than lactic acid, leading to a more complex taste with an airier crumb. Other men milled around behind them. Watching, did they surmise Turner's obsession? With each jerk of his head he resumes slurping at the dish he can't put down.

Sinful fudge, true vanilla Bernadette fake-climaxed for All-Natural Breyers Lite Frozen Dessert in 1992 *I'm cheating!* Once my then-boyfriend H. and I got both of us fucked by a massage therapist, short with a prize cock, who rubbed down our IT bands, sore calves, and stiff buttocks. He kissed with a particularly ferocious suction which I returned to with the insistence of a cat after a synthetic mouse tied to a wand. Losing focus on H. I made out with our fling, repetitious and obsessive. Edging towards a crisis he told me to open my mouth. I wilded my orgasm into my trusting boyfriend, but my primary satisfaction came from the heavy cock lacing the back of my throat with fetid cum.

The longer the rise, the more the acid produced by the yeast's anaerobic fermentation will transmute into a flavorful bread—or else the overlong proof will collapse the protein structure, dissolved in the surfeit of acid. There in the notorious basement I went down on Mike till I smelled like Mike's cock. Then he kissed me with enough force and suction that he smelled like Mike's cock too. Reader, if you had been present you would have been spritzed with Mike's cock like a fine dense mist!

Dinner's ready,
Turner

SLY RED DOLLS

Dear Niel—

Let's play never have I ever, I'll start. I've never had my letters intercepted but I feel so enthused I don't mind, you pick up my threads and stitch them into other garments. I'm good for nothing but skewering an image and sex in the future tense. So let's go: PrEP, ruffians, public sex.

You ask about the eroticization of HIV, I guess in reply: I don't ask after any lover's status, the privilege of taking blue pills the size of hamsters. It's never got stuck but a Pure for Men tab did, or felt like it, no matter the coffee I guzzled, how furiously I gagged. You guess right anyways that something about *Bucks County's* sluttishness builds on the particular way to take a pill for anything that comes along. I love it like Jennifer North loves her sly red dolls, her comely yellows.

Never have I ever got cum in my eye, everywhere else is game—Kay interrupts to clarify: *her* hair's off limits, *mine* is not. I bareback less for an illusion of curated risk than I bareback for sensations:

- a top spurts, and perishes
- hot sludge funday
- I have to carry his baby
- so sa-a-d that you're creaming / it takes ti-i-ime to believe it
- the close friction around his cock loosens in a wash
- of slop dribbles out, the juices
- that boy over there wields a turkey baster
- i'm open, i'm open
- normal hole, juiced for dad
- breakfasted to an opposite mouth
- a nasal drip wrong side out
- up at 6 tomorrow g'night
- maybe taste it too

I could go one more and then I'd have a gross-out sonnet. Never have I ever been on SSRI's. Never have I ever had an anal orgasm, but I try all the time. Keep me coyly in your ear for winter.

A fellow traveler of the plein-air fuck,
Turner

THIS ONE'S INTO TEAL

Dear Stephen—

The horny grocery boy may be the god Pan in disguise. This one's into teal, birds, comics, actually he works at a printshop. It's Vermont all the way down, I've never been but I've got pictures of it, Vermont toilets in the background of a squat aggressively pink-tipped cock bobbing over Vermont water.

In the one I've got saved to my phone his chest looks like it's been stapled together very precisely: the front of his belly folds in at the center in one long seam from the solar plexus to just below the navel, a softball-sized bicep bugs out of his arm like uneven padding on an office chair. Except for lifting his shirt into a makeshift harness he'd be fully clothed right up to the copper-toned sunglasses perched in his hair, and gauges, thankfully small. Do Vermont's ribs beggar description? Hugging his hips, AMERICAN EAGLE in reverse, and an Uber ad at the bottom twice the length of his jeans.

Waiting for him to make the four-hour drive to New Jersey I guzzle water, check Facebook, check my texts, edge, think about the word spooge. *Why Vermont* everybody wanted to know. I remember you did too, anticipating the scandal and then the likely tedium of the shacked-up weekend plus Labor Day. "Maybe he's bored," I suggested, and ate something to illustrate. Later he said he was, of married dick by trash piles and buggy rivulets and especially the print shop, where he didn't technically have time off. The morning before he showed up I picked out an especially scrunched pair of shorts, the globes of my ass (contraband) hung out of it and shone. *When he leaves* I texted Rylee *I'd better be raw like health-hazard meat.* I really wanted him to get the right idea. I'm neat like a rosewater cronut with sprinkles and a shave of ice. Who's gonna lap me up?

Driving on camera Vermont looks like he's whistling to a fly on his dick. *Taylor Swift visiting a children's hospital* the belt is as slack as his attention, divided between the road and his cock, which a furtive thumb and forefinger crush into his jeans. *Even if you didn't watch Scream Queens* one hand picks up rhythm, the other rests easy at 10 o'clock confidently arriving at—a school crossing, a stop sign, a delayed green light? Long enough to dribble with impressive restraint *you'll still want to take in season two only because John Stamos* to the base without smearing even a little plush synthetic car seat fur and its tidy hotel-carpet blues and greys.

By 1 AM I played through every IG story. *How do you feel about a scene* I texted. *Oh?* and a smirking cat emoji. Yeah. *Like instead of I meet you in the parking lot you buzz up here and whip it out in the hallway.* Three more cats. Uh, sick. I zoomed in on the peaks and gullies of his egg-carton abs. *Neighbors?* my phone buzzed. *Are all squares* I reply, *who gives a fuck.* I shrill out of sleep at 3 AM to the alarm bell chime and buzz him upstairs. I'd imagined after weeks of reciprocal nudes I'd be slobbering wet but as I listened to the elevator brakes give and clamp my throat went dry and my balls huddled scooped against my perineum like two squirrels keeping warm.

Which brings me to his balls. Somehow in the jerkoff videos they'd squeeze tightly into his inguinal canals, grouped shyly around his cock looking more like identical growths, a sandcastle artifice packed by muddy adolescent hands. Lower limit amber briefs, upper limit amber balls. Where in this schema amber socks? Erupting onto his stomach he dodges the question.

Hello to the birthday party public of the apartment complex, cool stoops, warm beer. It is exactly 3:19 AM. *What's good* he smirks over a wakeful cock. Top of the morning to me too. His balls edge distortedly out over teal briefs, AMERICAN EAGLE waistband. The telltale *thunk-woosh* of another door opening startles me out of a reverie of delivery cock, I pull him into the apartment where he kicks off his jeans. Lean legs, little teal socks.

Which his nudes had amply prepared me for. Here, flat on a creamy bedspread legs apparently vulnerably in the air, he jerks his cut pole. Briefs open wide as if to catch, but wouldn't you know? He jets on his stomach with the kind of energy that suggests he's been saving it up—for me, his personal piggy bank. I say this even as I look again and again at the cum cooling into translucency in the navel it fills and, by 0:43, overflows. That's what the briefs tell me. The socks, that he has a fixation, which is just the precision of desire made stretchy, elastic, teal or amber, ERICAN EAG, ILFIGER, TOM.

Okay, the stranger danger, the dick breakfast, the neighbors—I fibbed. Here's the real story. I really did close my eyes but fifteen minutes later I was striding out to the parking lot where I sized him up in the privacy of cars, nights, mosquitoes, and the buzz of a Mercer County, NJ road. He looked just like his photos and a little shorter, so I kissed him hello. It lasted a good half-minute—"You kiss like a cocksucker," he offered. Without a comment on the complex's disrepair he followed me upstairs and indoors, where he bred me till the carpet burned my wrists and arms into a welter of bruising. Taking his cock—on the shorter side, but pleasantly thick, and hard as anything—was easy and joyous. He had the kind you don't even need to relax for, you just let him rock into you. See? You get all silly over the translation from pixel to sphincter but there he goes hitting the right note with confidence, precision and ease.

He pulled out and told me to get on the bed with my legs in the air, to circle a finger around my head. "Slower," he said, "tell me when it starts to burn." I did, and then he ate my hole—sloppy, rest stop burger, fries, coke, lettuce. Outside crickets shrilled into a swampy 2 AM, inside he smacked and mumbled his appreciations into my hole. Of course, I'm a pornographer, I believe in the torment of desire—so I stopped teasing my cock for his benefit, grabbed his hair and held him back until he returned me the needy gaze of a pet. This control is out of the question for him to relinquish, or for me to backseat-drive. But in the interval of restraining him from my boy hole he blinked, fixed and one-sided. "Your ass tastes like pussy!" Flat iron, tree line, perineum. Fair enough, I supposed, I giggled, I let him in again. Runway, carpet, slip n' slide.

Irritation, bagels, road head. You asked me if I'd called him daddy, well I was going to until he confessed he'd rather be my cat. All things and one long weekend. We were going at it in the kitchenette when I gave him his first hit of poppers, a minor practice new to him and probably an affront to somebody somewhere. A sluice of vision, a slowed but more deliberate rhythm to his fucking, I guess every cohabitant could hear us like pipes snapping or the intrusions of a radiator when somebody adjusts the heat. He wore boots, I wore sneakers, and then I was naked except for the sneakers and the impression of having done something extravagant.

Halfway through the weekend, feeling like a break from our elaborated fucking, I trussed him up to the shower curtain rod, got out my camera, and started to play. The AMERICAN EAGLE waistband indexed handsome cock redolent of pine needles and cold mountain air. The PETSMART collar said drive me to the movies. His cock bobbed, short and stupendously hard, over tile and bathmat. Flipping him around, it came as a surprise he had basically no ass to speak of—I must have been so fixated on his pelvic lines I forgot to check. So when he admitted he thought I had lied about my name I felt doubly betrayed. "Turner sounds fake, like porn-fake," he said between forkfuls of potato and scallion.

Did I forgive him when he, following instructions, pulled me into a sloppy embrace in front of a public library and a local Panera? Oh, Stephen. That's for you to decide.

Turner.

SHUT YOUR MOUTH

Turner likes the speakers.
Halogen lamps, granite,
glass, kitchen island, another.
Doug looked husky, now
he just looks rich. His condo

prevails far and wide, and there's the highway:
jammed, strips of red and white.
Like, uh, tuna?
Turner liked that, the sushi,
ceiling mirrors, the condo's milling puppies,

the parking garage, the Maserati
stack of 20s by the toaster.
Later he'll slide some over
his ass and thighs. He'll pout
for shits, think about a bra

to hold them, extract later still,
drop in a tip jar with a probably
forward kiss, probably
reciprocated. I'm famous, Turner
mouthed, after history has gone

to sleep. Good night to brushing
teeth, barstools, sushi.
Turner, bossy bottom:
Shut your mouth. The mirror
gets all coy and shit.

THE VAMPIRE MORTGAGE

Dear Stephen,

A woman with generously fake hair, is that so bad to want? October polishes its cinematic knives, I miss you even in the ambience of tasteful death. My taste isn't recherché, not at all. Every night I watch another's murder scene with another's taste—the Criterion Collection yelps but it's my faint body wadded up like a can of mountain dew. Let my plaque read *Turner, a shudder of the 'burbs. He had chilblains on his chilblains, perky nipples and no original thought.* Stick it up in the garage where all your friends go wow and shit.

I'm twenty-one or twenty-two when I meet the Vampire Mortgage. He's tall and feudal, and wears a feudal wig. Weekends he plays in a Neil Young cover band. The Vampire Mortgage isn't evil, a fastidious respecter of property. He texts a full twenty-four hours before entering the apartment, but he always gets invited in.

I'd like to go the way that one chick does in Suspiria with a rafter precise like a draftsman's triangle gashing her from A to B and a hypotenuse the length of her sternum to her pubic mound. Even in death you can't get away from family or student loans—that's the movie version. We know better, but the thought loosens up a bowel.

Things to do in the land of the dead:

- die, apparently
- misplace your passport
- appeal to a bureaucrat over same
- get written up for noise complaints
- dodge border guards, apparently

I feel like insisting on death's finality. The dead think otherwise, and they aren't affable pets about it, with gently removable jowls. Don't you wanna know all about me? I sure as hell would. Last week I opened the incision on my forehead and blinked through a bright red curtain, like my vision had installed an on-off blood switch. *Old blood or new blood?* a nurse asked over the phone. She sounded stressed but I didn't know how to answer the question; blood on, blood off, then it got in my mouth, a burst piñata of sensation. Old blood, past its sell-by date, in unseemly splotches on the bathroom tiles. I went in there to drip like scheduling my own execution and summary clean-up; I'd like it to be enthusiastically gross but also not to shit or piss myself, can one of you make that happen for me? The verb that comes to mind is "spurt."

I intend to maintain the dignity and spectacle of my own production, and still smell good. Some of these stains, come to think of it, are corn syrup from a blood capsule, the costume "sexy murder bunny." All night long I invited men to pull my tail, then one did. He climbed inside my warren to the warm rank fragrance of nibbled seeds and bunny shit.

The Vampire Mortgage wears a hat, which he sometimes touches with cool methodical movements. He's double-jointed and likes to prove it at parties. Although he can be photographed, if he notices a camera pointed his direction he'll billow out of the frame like soot. Then he'll break your neck, impersonally.

Everybody gets to be sexy, like everybody gets to die. Warhol said something like that only he's, admit it, a nihilist, we don't do the same drugs. Here's a fable: a girl grows a wolfish tail in the subdivisions. It's probably Brampton, Mississauga, Etobicoke, but why not Bergen County? Horny teens frot it up with pork swords, get periods and check out on screen like library books. The tail wiggles on its own, wired into a cultural nervous system from which it receives its tense and intermittent pulses. It wants to see the world, and grows and grows, wobbling under Target panties, taped to a hairy teenaged leg. Finally it develops its talents and dashes to the high school, dragging its snarling occupant along: *bump, bump*. Some bodies later she checks out too, an engine that designated itself for fuel and burns up part by oily part. Lights down on the hiddener abode, symmetrically boiled in its own slick.

Stephen I suspect that by day I'm a tower of glowing resentment and otherwise the process that keeps it alight. By origin or not I am "of" the city until I can't be—a choice, as choices go, made within constraints, one of which is surely beauty. Here's a fable about the mortal soul: Al Pacino takes an *Odyssey to the edges of city life*—Chelsea, where the camera finds that the differences between a cop and a leathery celebutante are null in a meat locker and pertinent everywhere else. In mascara and a yellow hankie he cuts a convincing figure, or is that his double? He enters the club on cop night, and finds himself persona non grata. Irony! The Hudson swells and shrinks with body parts, to nobody's satisfaction, not even the scriptwriters'. Pacino frames some schmuck and knifes him, twenty to life, they'll reduce the sentence if he fesses up. The cop's wife waits for him on a beautiful soundstage. *One day this whole city's gonna explode*, and that's still true. Some say decadent, a coded gripe in moral flannel, looking down its moral nose.

I'm giving the Vampire Mortgage a ride over the Verrazano when I learn he has neither a mother nor a father. *I was created* he admits, considering his bleached fingers *but then I bought him out*. When I express my jealousy he feigns surprise.

Here's a fable with the ring of truth. A jock lets a known queer slobber on his dick. Plugging into the hole at the bottom of his need he wonders if he'll catch something. When the sissy blabs the jock shows up at school to find his buds having flown the coop of his friendship. Dumped on the floor, the contents of his locker accuse him too. What can he do but point a meaty finger? These balls won't suck themselves, and you know how queers like to plug the hole at the bottom of their resentment. To prove it he roughs up his erstwhile hookup. His misdirection takes effect, the spoiled contents of a different locker accuse him too, like a wife who knows where he's been. The little guy takes the burden off his conscience and leaves the school district, or something. He doesn't show up in the dark with a knife for his tormentor, but wouldn't that be nice?

Double nice for that, and every other petty vengeance, and every major one too. Here's one that isn't mine to tell. It isn't even the teller's, really, who got away to talk about it. A woman goes home with the one straight guy in the room, medium-cute and comfortable, he has his own place and says he'll tip. The cab takes them way, way off the subway, and the molly wrinkles the corners of her attention. They have a boring sort of sex until they don't, then he pokes around her pussy like a bad check. *Did you have an operation*, her trick demands. Then: *Tell the truth*, and, luridly, *I'm not some kind of faggot*. She lies, fakes indignation to pull the shades down on her fear, shouts and shouts till he relents and gets her a car. It's meanwhile started to rain, and she walks out with his umbrella. When she tells this story to friends the umbrella takes center stage—*how did I get this? funny you ask*—till she takes a trip and it busts unsturdily in her suitcase.

The Vampire Mortgage lives in a large house up Victory Hill in Staten Island, plenty old, with a verandah that buckles away from the street. He invites me in although he doesn't have to. Naturally, he lives alone: no roommate, no child back from piano lessons, and

nothing that clobbers his windows at night with stones
or clumps of sod. He keeps rockin' in the free world,
up the grand staircase and into his cabinet of boutique
deaths.

What's the lesson? Stephen I sometimes get the sense that
white queers crave distinction; the monster thing, like Jackie
says, the drapery of a special coat without anything to invite
the concerted attention of a cop. Then it gets real: do you
choke? As for distinction, there are real villains and we know
them by their zip codes, their uniforms, or their fancy fucking
backpacks.

I don't keep myself off this list except how anybody can. In
the future we'll shed our rent like onion skins. I want to blow
the roof off the world as much as anybody, with half the spite.
I also want to get fucked. What do these have to do with each
other? This my nasty, gentle gift.

Lights out,
Turner

RIPE NEW YEAR

Dear Niel—

I haven't written back to you because, in a word, work—the first time I wrote this sentence it was work and then work and family, the ferments of a sour mood. The poem "goes back to the train it's been riding," Zach said, though lately it's mostly sleep and seeing the same conductors and no poems. I'll fight Jersey with my fists, I'll tell you all about it next to luscious suggestions. I'm on a bus now too, no mass transit spared in the gasps between these sentences. Space is very cruel and now it's winter you can't avoid it, it's pay to play and I put on my coat out of spite, while underneath the same fabrics skimp on what I love.

Is bareback our theme by way of allegory? All I've got is men, poems, work, rent, disgust and transit, you're the darling of my anal obsessions. Last week a trick held my hair over his choice (expensive) blow and asked if he could skip the condom, I don't know why I agreed. Then it was four or five AM and I felt wide, my phone said "wife," awake, with an ass ready to burst like a seltzer bottle dropped down a flight of stairs.

He wasn't Daddy but I said so. For a tip nearly anybody could waste my time, all I've got is this body to ruin and somebody else's grillwork staircase to clamber up, to creep out the doctors and goodnight mom and dad, and also for luxurious things, faux-fur gloves, chocolate, drinks, a muppetty coat. Which equation feels like it hesitates on the "innocence of scandal"—your letters innocent too, lapping up excretion with the trusting curiosity of something small and teething.

Don't think I ever met an excretion I didn't like in theory, though—bravo—your sonnet pushed the limits of even my

abstract guts. In 1968 Cecilia Vicuña wrote PHOOZ PHOOZ
about her boyfriend's asshole, and elevated the craters of
his nose. Included, a gross-out sonnet for Niel, of a vacant
douched morning, it plays the same tune. Forgive these
sentences their textures, or lap them up like dogs their up-
chucked kibble:

hello, my husband of the grocery
aisle where there's clams
stuffs a haunch, beef, a forearm
down my throat to tickle the womb
M.I.A. plus a side of "creamed spinach,
poached eggs" from concentrate
murder my crotch it sounds like mmmnngggg
dead as a dick, R.I.P., an -ectomy
feeds me his watch too
now who'll call me for dinner?
gnight bellies, hello golden syrup!
I'm *nobody*'s kibble, Tammy
Wynette asks if I'm sure, oh hell.
Phooz phooz for the ripe new year

x (phooz) o (phooz),
Turner

TRAVEL ADVISORY FOR CONSTANCE AUGUSTA

1. A DEVICE

Dear Connie—

I expect at any moment the scaffolding on this façade will collapse to reveal either nothing or an attractive hood ringed with fur. Underneath the hood is Turner, a persona in a bag. I suppose this is like replying to the noirish gun at my temple that I am not Kay Gabriel, minor internet personality, but I am the stinker holding the gun. Should I say cocking? That's my schtick, like sticking a tongue depressor in my mouth in public and going *AAAHHHHHH*. Turner can't come to the phone right now, can I take a message?

Here I vamp for our curious spectators. I'm vexed at the tendency of writers living and dead to use transsexuals as the window-dressing of social decay, a metonym for public space seductively in crisis. Surely this is cousin to these same icons' habit of pursuing a literary drag—you can be a Sosostris, slice up Warholia in retrospect, act in poems like you're very famous and everybody cares about who you're screwing and how—but not really a consequence of it unless you don't think transsexuals read. I wrote *Bucks County* on a diagonal from trans literature, because I don't appreciate being first outed then hailed as pretty but dumb or hopelessly abstract, which I expect will continue until I scare off the haters pornographically. Let's say these are one and the same coin: a literature of the city, dicking around in the afterimage of modernism, in which transsexuals always mean something else; a private literature of recognition. Let the motherfuckers further consider that their metaphor might come unsexily to life and, living, need housing in that glamorous, impoverished city, and testify to something other than an origin story that could be blurbed as important.

I want to earfuck the device, and I want you listening over the phone. Last night I dreamt of myself, Lana Turner, a milky sentence, lumps in my mouth. I tell Jo *Turner is a way to seduce my friends without having to deal with the consequences*. I tell Stephen *Turner is a heteronym of the author*. Shiv calls me "boyish, girlish." Dear Connie. What'll I call you? Come back tomorrow, I'll be more specific.

Meanwhile halfway through this poem I moved from a shitty apartment in an affluent Jersey town where I was—and at the time of writing and rewriting this letter, am still—employed for a low wage to a gentrification box in Flatbush. I thought that living with the tech girls of Brooklyn would solve my cash problems, but actually it means colliding daily with their halo of money, a queasy imposition against the tenuous statuses of wage, immigration, and healthcare of those I love most, including myself. "I just need something, I need a third credit card," my roommate says. But I can't move, I derive too much sadistic pleasure from the quarrels of Money with her live-in boyfriend. Then again if I have written this poem prolifically it is largely because of my currently lush relationship to the working day: for a brief time I have needed to clock in nowhere, not even a classroom, a luxury I take with a vengeance when my employer only recently threatened paycheck, insurance, housing and visa status over a flubbed translation. You understand: that if I, Turner, a heteronym of the author, am luscious, viscous and sly; if I schlep from fiberglass core to weedy suburb with minor need, or a hatful of pleasure, and tell you all about it; if I lie, rob and insinuate it's because I'm a cheat, a villain and a leading lady—oh, here's Turner again, would you like to speak with him?

Dear Connie. Turner is a delicate temptress and he can hear you. He's spitting, he's out for blood, he won't put on his coat, he's strict in his dogmas and in this he resembles a boyfriend, he's lax in his principles and in this he resembles everybody. He instructs me to attach the following statement.

2. THE STATEMENT

A QUEEN IN BUCKS COUNTY IS A SERIAL POEM. IT TAKES THE FORM OF AN EPISTOLARY SERIES COMPOSED BY ME, TURNER, A HETERONYM OF THE AUTHOR, A PERSONA IN A BAG. I ADDRESS MYSELF TO SOME RECIPIENTS (THE LETTER), SEVERAL DEDICATEES (THE LYRIC), AND A SEVERE BURNING GRUDGE OR TWO. I, TURNER, WILL MAKE YOU HORNY, MAD OR ENTHUSED. I WILL MAKE YOU SQUAWK OR COME. YOU'LL LEAVE THE LIGHTS ON WHEN YOU CHOKE.

3. TRAVEL ADVISORY FOR CONSTANCE AUGUSTA

"PLEASE DON'T SIT OR STAND ON BAGGAGE CAROUSEL." Connie this sign is just as cruel as it is imperative, especially for the kind of carousel that doesn't disgorge its bags from a significant chasm but loops around in the shape of a boot and the same bags reemerge from tantalizing black car-washy plastic—it could be any bag emerging but it wasn't mine. Yes, this must be a letter for Connie, I'm in transit! So is my bag, but it's not with me, it transited Lake Ontario in a different craft, so why not run off with someone else's bag? If really my concern is that I lost some mass of clothes and makeup and underwear, maybe all my makeup and underwear, could I saunter into the night with a stranger's adequately sized wheelie bag and forego the shirts, jeans, boots, and briefs I really like? I'd have a bag for sure but there I'd be without underwear walking out into Queens where it really matters! When my bag returns from its adventure I might well kiss it or do a cartwheel. I'd cartwheel into the path of a bus. Then I'd be screwed. Oh, the carousel is starting its warning farts. Now I could ride!

Love always,
Turner

SHKLOVSKY 2

Dear Stephen—

I dream of vanilla bean. There I was in my little pink shoes, my little pink hat, my little pink gown about to say I do to my big bright groom, Viktor (the groom, not the hat), when he turned into another boyfriend—oh, I lose count of laundry.

Cam informed me gravely that you can't invent a dream, but in this lighter wash of jeans he looks like my dad crossed with a young Christian Bale.

"Can I write you into *Bucks County*?" I asked him. "Sure." "By name?" "Yep. Yeah." So I did. How should I start? In my little pink tee, my little pink shorts, my little pink boots, my enormous appetite.

Noon and night Elsa feeds her trout, Constanza. It lays eggs that never go anywhere, neither meeting nor workshop. They may not feed themselves, but several grow ingenious at petty theft for all the not budging out of place. By the third *how much* she quietly masturbates over the phone.

Sometimes Viktor is as bashful as if, climbing the shelves, he'd knocked over something loud and formal. Or he bounds over to me clearly desiring to be picked up.

It's clear from the letter that the author is suffering from an *idée fixe* that I hesitate to call "yearning." I lost my other headphone just in time to hear several televisions in contingent harmony. Is this the realism of the public sphere? On a recent and totally beautiful morning Cam fucked my face on repeat. It got me thinking about the best time of day for it, a question I started asking friends and strangers: what's her favorite time for a tryst? Morning, night and party hours each got their share but my vote went to the afternoon, when you get a real sense of the day going to waste in the prolonged shift from one arrangement to another. I suspect that here I'm disappointing someone but Stephen I feel certain it isn't you.

Most of these arrangements terminate identically, a guy rocking into my face with the casual eagerness of opening the mail in search of a check. Does he ever fall away in disappointment?—oh, Viktor, I bragged again.

Viktor has knocked over a pumpkin. "Quit clowning around!" I said. "Shut up and kiss me!" Elsa, oversudsed, takes refuge in the body of a cat.

Cam knows it better than maybe anyone, so when I purr at him to fuck my face he obliges with enthusiasm and a little ceremony. *What an obliging man* Liam agreed *what a handsome cock!* It's visually delighting: long enough to impress without discomfort, a perfect smooth head coquettishly uncut, attractive low-hanging balls that drape his perineum when he reclines louche in the sun amid complaints of feral cats from the yard. I say he's used to it but there go the muscles in his face—now tense, now relaxed, and expressive enough for two.

One night I dream that Mike's cat Ezra is harboring the ravenous soul of one Ezra Loomis Pound, who can be appeased only by a large loan and snacks. But I'm mistaken, it's the Ezra from Pretty Little Liars, the Ezra from *Vox*, and the Ezra from Vampire Weekend squabbling over whose turn to wash up in an unlivable homestead.

Pleasure in a reliable procedure has its own surprise. An aesthetic emerges out of the gap of repetition. I don't think I can sit still especially long. So is my appetite especially arranged around sustaining the longue durée? Maybe, but monotony has its own charm. I clue into the formula for *Gossip Girl*, seasons 3-6: the intrigue builds in discrete moments until minute 22, when the teens gather at one disastrous party; calamities, Florence Welch cameo.

Cam picks up rhythm, pushing his cock into my mouth with quick little tugs. I make eye contact—pleadingly?—then methodically take the wheel, one hand firmly on the shaft, the other applying gentle pressure to the base of his cock or rolling his balls in alternation. Another cat yelps in the backyard, somewhere construction. Cam thrusts more urgently yet until I tell him to pull out and jack off, to shoot on my face till it looks like an exhibition of melted wax figurines. He quivers continually for a half-minute before spooning his cum into my mouth with a forceful adoring touch. This part we've rehearsed enough he springs to it without instruction, and it's the directness with which he charts a narrative, as forthright as "I want to taste my cock on your mouth," that pushes me over the edge of my own orgasm, expelling a milky puddle over my crotch and navel. After he comes he strokes himself absently, a last scrim of cream moving with his foreskin to the head of his cock and back until it's rubbed into the skin like soymilk. The word *striation* jams in my head, then Ezra Loomis, dick apartment, Takis Fuego.

Little pink husband on a little pink freeway. I haven't told any of the girlfriends where he's taking me for the weekend—no Samantha to expunge my domestic bliss like badly-aimed milk, no untoward Kyle MacLachlan.

Sometimes he leaves a sluice over my anal pubes, then gobbles it up and regifts it with relish. Or if I've nestled vertically on his cock and he drips soaking onto his own crotch it's my turn to nose over his fragrant skin like a Swiffer pad. Or if arched back as if for the audience of casually interested household cats I jizz on my own belly and ribs I spoon up my mess and present it on a couple fingers like scooped illicitly from an uncooked batter, a surrogate for Takis. Holding our juices like a wash I like to push them into his mouth and receive it back, yanking ropey strands between us in a sour tug-of-war in which cum stands out from saliva more by viscosity than flavor—if you taste it, it's already broken apart, you start from scratch. Practice is a meticulous obsession, so one refractory period later he breeds me languorously, shoots onto my ass, and snowballs me the results: quick, clean, delicate.

I'm no femme fatale. I'm no typist. I'm Turner, red and sweating. My credit is shit and I'm going to marry Viktor the Russian Formalist, Viktor the pornographer, Viktor who writes me letters, and Viktor in the absorptive body of a cat.

CAM You can't invent a dream, but you can lie extravagantly. What happened to your shirt?

TURNER I shredded it for the delight of the audience. All I've got left is this jockstrap's athleticky stripe.

CAM That's touching. [*Fingering it.*] And the audience? [*Mouthing the jockstrap, he listens intently*]

TURNER The scandalized presence at the Elsa Triolet mudfight, replete with real triolets. [*He yanks the jockstrap off until it droops from one ankle.*]

[*Cut to the fight. Elsa thinks of striation, Turner of Takis Fuego.*]

CAM Tragic endings—at least a broken heart— are inevitable in an epistolary novel, but not in so many words final. So too the strong rewriting of form as content. [*He begins to move the foreskin on his softening cock.*] Everything grey at night, not just the cats. What's the time? [*Turner, sucking on Cam's fingers like a toothbrush, declines to answer.*]

Later I say I should grab the bus and head back to my place for the evening. "Sure, if you're sure. More coffee?" he asks, and he's already pouring some. It's called realism, you know? Dear Stephen. Viktor is making my slippers talk to the weather again.

I called in sick,
Turner

A QUESTIONNAIRE FOR THE READER

1. What teenaged mistake do you intend to repeat?

2. Name 5 habits you intend to give up. Is Turner on that list? Why or why not?

3. Tell me an origin story involving first written then visual pornography.

4. "I know from my own boyhood in a Lutheran church, and from sleeping with the minister's son, that church activities can be as exciting as the St. Mark's Baths." Relate an activity as exciting as the St. Mark's Baths.

5. Rank and describe your three favorite climaxes. Relatedly, what's the only way to fly?

6. Pick a sonnetician. Write a sonnet in your chosen style, using only material generated in the previous questions. Enclose with love to Turner at the following address—

SHUT YOUR MOUTH

Dear diary: Turner's full of TV words.
"Party," he doesn't till he does,
and it's a super couple
percs plus whatever Daddy's
getting, tonight handsome Drew.

Ruddy, tank top, jeans, implements,
intrigue. Winsome couple,
Drew with a smirk,
Turner slurping on his pits.
A foot off Turner smelt the beer

breathing on its own. Tight hairs,
choice musk. *Bite down*
Drew bosses. I'm somebody's
drama queen. I'm a TV
guide. On oxy Turner

tripped between moments
like a kid. That's all for pits,
and the implements come off,
the soundtrack cues,
and everything, like, blisters.

Drew whales on his thighs
till it gets old, flips him wrong
side up, and goes to town. *Shut
your mouth.* Turner expects to taste
his own ass, and why not?

BATH 1

Stephen—

One thing is as good as another—does this offend you?

Daddy's boys are fighting instead of kissing—does *that* offend you?

The Tristan chord resolves, and the boys kiss. The cat sniffs Cam's briefs—me too!

I am a pornographic user—what could that mean? If people like to look at you, doesn't that mean you win? In the bath I'm not supposed to take I soap everything, even my armpits.

Have you ever looked at an armpit?

I'm being obtuse. I meant to send a questionnaire! I did to Cam, and now he's part of the poem. Does that offend you? Name your sources of offense from one to a billion. *One*-one thousand, *Two*-one thousand—No, you're unflappable. I'm a bird, I'm a cake! I'm Turner. Have we met?

What happened since my last letter? I traveled, cried, fucked. I lost my bag in transit, I broke up with lineation—that's a lie. The same night I lost my bag I hosted a party. It was New Year's, actually the night before. The boys showed up with all the light step of murdering the past without the hipster frenzy of picking the right party for it. One thing's as good as another. A punk ate my ass between the urinals and the piss tub. I didn't remember we'd fucked before until I rode his face like teenagers in a playground encounter stiff old swings, the seat's too small so you stand. Then your fingers get stuck in the chains. He chewed my taint, he smacked at my hole, a week's stubble irritated my ass and the base of my nut sack, then it was midnight. Men screwed up their bodies to squeeze past us and pee. I raised a leg, I rested it on his back, my balls and cock draped his forehead like a fleshy visor. When he tried to blow me I brushed him back to where he belonged. A kid tries to get a toy out of a lollipop—*three*-one thousand, *four*-one thousand.

One thing's as good as another. On the uptown 5 a punk, a different one, held a cat nestled dopily in his lap, a little ginger creature—the animal dozed, I didn't see it until I sat down. Then I watched it over the edge of my book. Actually I watched the owner hold it absently. Dry hands, medieval flop of hair. He listened to EDM, I nodded along. Exiting at 14th St. the urge gripped me to scoop it up and carry it off the train for my own, to make its champion dart after me and show me his face. If I had a type I'd be twee. So why bother encountering the most impressive boy you've ever seen, at least until you get on the train home and do it again? You won't know if they watch till the lights flash and you win. Then everybody gapes, your sweepstakes are the cats of New York City, you can double or nothing to get Yonkers too. Every boy regards you with a nauseating dent in his cheeks.

I'm having mine filled—then I'll be round as a loaf!

Nine-one thousand. *Ten*-one thousand,
Turner

LAP JUICE

Dear Niel—

Do you remember what your ass looked like at 18? I can't, or my piecemeal face, youth is a sham—even the vengeful overgrown ex-teenaged Turner agrees and I'll bust a Rimbaldian nut about it. Mostly I think "twink" is a funny word. Outside the window cheery horns—it is January, and I'm chaste and sober, no, I'm screwing myself to my tidy sheets! I'll milk the cream out of the calendar, I'll let it drown in retail.

What do you do on New Year's? Too bad for the singlet daddies but I guess you didn't get fastidious and schtup away with them at midnight. What do I do, even? Two years back a crush bucked his quivering orgasm into my mouth. A medical case with a crushed bruise for a pelvis, I couldn't really walk or stand, but we jerry-rigged a fuck, determined to crush December into a powder of sensation. I lay on my back making drowsy eye contact until he shook as if I'd left him outside with the motor running.

Last year I think it happened in the street. I've done it on rooves (roofs?), I've done it watching the dumbest fucking shows, burlesque, rave, circuit party, you crash somewhere and in the morning head back under a smush of eyeshadow. At nineteen or twenty I wrapped my legs around some regular who knew the bartenders, a sober (he said) water sign with his own apartment who licked me clean, rolled over and passed out dreaming, he said, of showers. I tried to impress, thought I ended up a disappointment but really I was probably just young and empty.

Now I'm regular, metabolic, enviable. I'm comelier now than 18—well who isn't. (Comely, another for your non-adverb

collection.) An ex-friend, 21, freaked at "aging out of sex."
I hope he's sagging now, but he's not worth the thought. A
gross-out sonnet to topple the jutting hipbone shits, and up
with thighs and backs and stuff:

Get off loser, I'm your bravo
bully in athletic shorts whose
lint you'd snort off a toilet seat
and whose pits
you'd probably take out loans
to huff—
beer, bacteria.
I'll die with heaps of laundry
mildewed in crummy weather.
In this poem I do it twice,
aged into my extremely
handsome looks.
I call them "chunks of bowel"
and "lap juice." I call them candy.

I've also done it in my own bed, where last night I dreamt
the dream called *chunks of bowel*. I dreamt the dream called
spooge, and *dissociate at the 24-hour laundromat*. I dreamt the
dream called *nobody else washes my clothes*. I conked out with
a Percocet.

When I'm thirty-seven, will I have Nicolas Cage to take me
out to *La Bohème* with my hair like wings or curtains? Please
say yes,

Turner

BATH 2

Dear Connie,

Letter for letter, bath for bath. You anticipate my figure for camp decadence—uncanny, except for talking every day, like a lover who preempts your sentences and exacerbates them. How did the bathtub get here? How did I? Today I shuffled through the Kosher market at Empire and Brooklyn. In a social realist novel of the 80s this scene would have featured a telling social encounter in which I'd either succeed or fail. In a movie I'd have shoplifted. In a Belle and Sebastian song I'd be pregnant. In *Bucks County* like the awkward confines of my life I dissociate, crawl home, act out in a warm envelope. I'm largely indifferent between my bed and hot water except that one of them is illicit, my roommates' bathroom with the expensive soaps and makeup brushes and the exquisite Chanel bottles on the vanity. For shame, Turner: what kind of Gomorrist, I mean, flâneur, retreats to her chambers? What kind of enthusiast of glances? Well, shut up, it's January, nothing sexy ever happened.

Or is that right? A couple days ago en route to the Sterling St. 2/5 some teens said faggot very loud. You know what I mean when I say they're not wrong, a white queer in Flatbush is a walking icon of rent going up, I get why someone would look and say so. It's a telling social encounter after all, but there's no success or failure—on one side of a schoolyard fence a white queen with a big pink bag, on the other Black teens notice who comes in and out of the subway.

The irony is that I couldn't afford to live in my building either without Money and her boyfriend shouldering most of the rent. I have fantasies that this intense friendship of ours will culminate in a home—have we written ourselves into a sitcom? There won't be any dying young and we'll have time for writing or to do whatever, masturbate, mutual childcare (will there be children?), time at the beach, no more Januaries. I got this image from somebody else, does it matter?

Except that it's predicated however distantly on the family. In the bath I wasn't supposed to take I watched a dire riff on *Bake-Off*, the same thing only more so: in place of benign pâtissières dialing grandkids when through to the semis the whole family trundles on set, planting Swedish flags on meat-balls, reciting the stages of a risotto, serving up for the judges in their converted warehouse condo, Shepherd's Bush. Even the cake's in tiers, eh? BE NICE OR LEAVE, blonde wood from a sanded mouth. Spacious counters, chocolate, rice, martinis, kitchen island, poppers, Tina, is this thing on? I agree that the beautiful is beautiful, a fenced playground of peach and apri-cot. I write not in consolation but a shared grievance, brood-ing in now-tepid water, out for blood. "The judges must now decide which family to put through." It's not a game you win, but some lose it by shitting in the sauce. Love from me, and Kay, sharpening her shrewish claws—

Turner

THE NAMES OF FAMOUS BEACHES

Dear Jo—

What do I have to say that Liz Phair didn't, or my anxiolytics? I started writing you this letter in a California suburb, except for the vegetation and the high winds it could've been anywhere, like the non-place of an airport mall. Actually I think we were next to LAX. Anywhere was a delivery coming in overhead, and the office buildings: Siemens, for instance, World Courier Inc., and Air One Logistics, Air Sea Forwarders, Plexis Freight, Las Lilas Coffee, and a 24-hour Ralph's, where I walked through the aisles and read the back of the cereal boxes at night, hoping to catch my own appetite. Who says you can't be a flâneur in LA—the cocoa puffs agree, I'm the center of this stoplight town, I've arrived but nobody knows it! I must remember to fire my publicist. Stephen speaks convincingly about Los Angeles, he says Santa Monica and it means something, to me it's just the names of famous beaches.

I guess what I'm trying to say is this whole past summer I wrote *Dear Jo*, I wrote it into other poems, I wrote it even when I wasn't writing you a letter and what I meant was *get me out*. Then Danny loaded me up in his car to watch the sunset plug the divots in Silver Lake. I'm a little snack in shorts, daddy's taking me to get a new leather something, this old choker I got from a boy in Chicago who I know won't stop bragging about it but I wouldn't kiss him anyways, you're the Chicagoan I would. Danny drove into the city and I slept in his car until the playlist flipped over to "Summertime Sadness." I think you like Lana more than I do—while I write this sentence, the morning before I'll see you, blond Bechdel, an Acker brat finally at home on the Lower East Side, she wafts onto the radio: *will you still love me*, etc. I'll credit the song everything it wants. You look like what the song wants to look like, Danny said, noticing a photo of me in the same shorts and choker leaning on a corrugated metal barn. I imagine having long hair to pile on top of a delicate mannequin face. Am I plastic enough for this plastic spot? We like Joni about the same, another Californian by design, and I like Spicer, for whom California isn't a choice but a long, inevitable grave. I like his letters especially, obsessive, reaching through a post office to brush Jim Alexander on his birthday. Dear Jo. I'm impressed with your precocious youth. Are you impressed with mine? Last night I dreamt about entering my credit score—I fudged the numbers high enough to fake it, adolescent no more. Will you love me when I'm as mature as my pleasant lies?

This week everybody's got something to say about pleasure and permissiveness, and the city, and who it's for. Yesterday I thought about the Club Kids appearing on Geraldo but today I'm thinking about the *Sex Series* that David Wojnarowicz made in 1989. I think David wasn't an especially technical photographer but *Sex Series* involved a series of darkroom tricks to produce prints that look like photographic negatives: a water tower, the Brooklyn and Manhattan bridges, a train speeding around a curve shot from above, like if Geena Davis and Susan Sarandon huddled on a cliff in the southwest with a Kodak, logistics, movement and storage in space. Each print's got a stamp of a contact image, a circular inset burnt onto the photo paper, mostly men undressed and fucking, lifted from the collection of a dead friend. David wrote about making the series to keep him company: putting fuck poems on the wall.

Could I disagree, washing in the varnish of what I do best? I want to kiss before hyperbole—that's more than a feeling. In June I backed my boyfriend into a rail yard, piled his cock out of his jeans and jerked him off between the freight cars, on a bed of shale. I guess I don't really know from rocks, or decency, but you and Liz know what I mean. We tightened in on each other, flush in case a window we couldn't see cut through the canopy behind us. Did I mention the L train going by, or the cemetery behind it? We stopped close enough to see the graveside decorations, pink and plastic, and then his cock stood over the hem of his clothes plump and upright like a water tower. If I'd drained it then and there I'd have kept a desert town in beverages for weeks. I put my free hand on the small of his back, pressing with a couple fingers into the top of the muscles on his ass. Will he arch his back for me? I couldn't tell, then he started to buck and whimper. Through an eyes-closed kiss I felt his blood pulse through the head of his cock, as if, had he climaxed right then, that's the fluid that would've slathered us both.

You know? I feel as gratified as if I'd finished too. A week later Canada took him back, and I started writing you letters I never sent, not even sleeping in the next room in Logan Square. Dear Jo. I think what I'm trying to say is I'd glam up with you before a hyperbolic event. I'm trying to throw my body at you, on a gurney of verbs, on a train in 1973. That's more than a feeling too, and I'm getting cuter all the time. Maybe one day I'll be a water tower, or a series of consequences. Write back and let me know all about you.

Love,
Turner

SHUT YOUR MOUTH

A caveat: there'll be another
body by the end of the poem.
Turner likes big gestures,
being talked about. He likes
it when Mike (different Mike)

scoops his ass up off
the mattress and shakes it like
a puppet, an electrocuted
puppet, a piece of ass
flapping in a puppet wind.

Mike shoots with the surprise
of a drain unplugging:
Gargle, suck, pop.
Did I come after him?
Sure. On the bus later

Turner's phone buzzed
and buzzed. There'll be another
body at the end of the call,
just one of those
talks and at the end you

really know somebody.
The stage lights fall and
everybody dies a bit,
shut your mouth,
then rallies manfully.

THE DREAM IN WHICH I APPEAR AS A POET

Dear Connie—

I shrilled at you in couplets the last time I moved, now I'm moving again. Smug victorious Money frustrates when and as she can, clamps down and plays a tug-of-war with the deposit. Chairs go aerial, dance speculatively for a while, then belch when they hit the ground. Dramatis personae: brokers, landlords, guarantors, Money, Zach, concerned boyfriends, once-friendly neighborhood cats hissing in cramped anticipation at bad unfamiliar smells.

Previously I panicked campily by way of Gore Vidal, who probably never had to pay rent in his life. You write ambivalently "against camp." The voice in which I sang about rent had a name. Her signature fragrance would've wafted notes of vanilla and citrus, the tang of buttercream. Now it's just me, Turner, who doesn't rhyme with any of his favorite verbs. I'm with you in the following key—what does camp have to say to rent strikes, landlords who drive tenants out of rent-controlled apartments by way of 24-hour construction and leaky ceilings unfixed after a dozen calls to 311, West Indian communities in Flatbush where new buildings rise on every block?

The mask had to come down sometime: fuck that.

I'm no allegorist. I'm a geographer. The cops who murdered Saheed Vassell for playing with a shower pipe work in a precinct at New York and Empire. They don't typically figure in the drama, but hurry in when windows get smashed, car taillights blink out or shop owners and new residents pick up the phone.

Last night I dreamt I fucked my landlord. He *still* charged me
rent.

From a kind of basement,
Turner

PERIPHERAL XO

Dear Stephen—

Everyone acts like they don't like it
as much as I do. Nearby, on screen,
someone moans convincingly in French.

All I've got is men,
poems, rent, work, disgust,
and transit. Don't you want
to come inside?

I moved from the shade
to the sun and still look
kind of shabby. Then I felt a shame

as drastic and exaggerated
as if I said I love you!
Men buy me things,

I return them for the cash.
Everyone here is beautiful,
remarkable, and sad.
I think I'm the only one,

though I missed a perfectly healthful
summer evening and didn't realize
until I had taken my glasses off

to encounter a suspect
friend, languorous, puffy,
derelict in Miami

like a personality. Trenton's been replaced by a toy!
I lost track of him in a pop of warranted anger.
Then he reappeared in the same outfit

on the other side of the country.
Still we caught up at the bar.
He has doctors now, he says.

Nice work if you can get it,
I tell Trent. Are there big baguettes?

I don't know, he admitted, I'm an amateur.
Next year I'll be a doctor,
I'll have my own penthouse.

He leans on the bar,
sultry and for a moment corrupt.
I'll have my own fitted sheet.

> TRENT   The most important thing in a relationship is
> trust. After sex, and hygiene, and earning potential.
>
> TURNER   You don't really mean that. What tentacle
> disaster's got hold of your all-American heart?
>
> TRENT   Says the bitch betrothed to money, if you
> went swimming with that rock you'd drown. I was in
> the Hamptons where they have penthouses too. The
> train didn't come for hours and I ran out of sand-
> wiches to distract me. Then I was replaced by a toy,
> identical except for his immaculate asshole.
>
> [THE VAMPIRE MORTGAGE and MONEY enter, wafted on
> the breeze of a local park and viscerally tan. Their faces

are full and relaxed. He's got a sumptuous dog, she's perched on a Coach bag. They put on masks—respectively, **MONSIEUR LE CAPITAL** *and* **MADAME LA TERRE**—*and seat themselves on plush local memberships.*]

MONSIEUR LE CAPITAL   Quiet doldrums by quiet streams—you were saying?

MADAME LA TERRE   We never go to the Jersey Shore. I'd call it budget.

TURNER   Are you two dating or just BFFs who show up at the same parties?

MME. LA TERRE   I am always by his side, at Red Lobster, in Port-au-Prince, in an oil flume.

M. LE CAPITAL   And I by hers though I rearrange them day, night and weekend.

TURNER   Your mustache looks familiar, have we met before? You look as if distorted by a screen.

M. LE CAPITAL   You will have encountered my deputies in the Bureau of Aesthetic Difficulty. You may be deputized yourself.

TURNER   I don't quite follow.

MME. LA TERRE   He means tenure, kid. What can you get in this watering hole?

TURNER   Anything with a twist. Anything with cinnamon or bitters. Anything prone to breaking that's also prone to liquidation. Probably an aperol spritz.

MME. LA TERRE [*rapping on the bar*] Tonic water sloshed over a cherry. His tab.

M. LE CAPITAL Sure. [*Explaining*] We cut loose after hours.

TURNER I remember now. You walk your dog Träger on the Home and Garden network. He has his own cooking channel, his own tree in the park.

TRENT [*shrugging*] Little pets. [*Then.*] Am I on glue or is that a chorus of middle management, dithering in key?

TURNER Probably, it's the right zip code. Round that bend there's a peripheral utopia, the springs run continually with grift.

THE CHORUS
My feet are awful sore
from standing desks and blonde
interiors but I'm puffy with
paid time off. The calendar
shat in my fauxcialite
hood, and I said "See you Tuesday!"
I bellyflop to Ridgewick for a bump.
I taste like Condé Nast wonder-twinsed with
Swiffer pads. I'll bop to be upscaled.
I am blissfully on call.

MME. LA TERRE Are they ramrodding the expressway? That's my cue.

[**MME. LA TERRE** *lifts herself from her stool. She unwraps her caftan and removes a miniature chapeau, from which cascades a tangle of impeccable finger-waved curls. She* *resembles* JESSICA RABBIT, *simultaneously vengeful and implicated.*]

JESSICA RABBIT   You never know when you'll need backup—I'd like a martini, very dry, and a seat for my personal saxophonist. My developments gobble yours for supper, and pick their teeth with heavy rail.

TRENT   You two make for mildly suspicious company, more an object of envy than opprobrium. Until, I guess, it's suppertime.

TURNER   Or your roots start to show.

JESSICA RABBIT   Don't start with me, you little monkey. You'd kill for this ass.

[TURNER's *continual smirk melts off his face and goes on vacation. He is replaced by a toy.*]

TURNER   As it should be, I feel much more casual! Who wants to take me for a spin?

TRENT   I'm out. The doctors turned up with a new speculum I am just yawning to try. [*To M. Le Capital*] Get me a car?

TURNER   Don't strain yourself. Anyone else?

GORE VIDAL, THE TOY   Me! Or actually I'll ride shotgun.

TURNER   And I drive stick. Beyond that bend a ribbed moraine, a recess of gay villainy.

PERIPHERAL UTOPIA   First I was a blank extension in an office. Then I was an institution, divided against myself with rail lines, much of it reserved for freight. Then I was a much-admired site of abject physical beauty, fishes without smell, collectives without guarantees. Toto never made it back from Oz, and my devouring earth conceals his dung into the present.

JESSICA RABBIT [*considering*]   Party.

Wouldn't you know, I slept it off.
Caught the bus in time

to encounter a wash of junk,
a derelict, a diva shrine.
Wasn't this what I was looking for?

Aggro make-out sesh in a setting
ripe for genre fiction,
a leading man, an audience on glue

Everything even the photographer
in neon and vinyl
No rain on a Sunday and the buses free

I am corrupt and going finally
to bed in an unprecedented way
as if I said I love you!

Peripheral xo,
Turner

YOU SAY WIFE

Dear Kay—

A letter in seven arguments.

1. ON LIES

In another poem a man compares me to pussy, and then it happens again. Rosario says straight men don't even *like* pussy, an attack so devastating I took it vicariously. Cause of death: personal correspondence. Do I care about straight men? The question is maybe misplaced.

Anyways they care about me. That coy interval between gays and trans women is good for a couple things, one of which is giving the lie to hetero protestations about themselves. I don't even believe them, culprits of their own desire, though as Cam says I think they believe themselves.

This thing is multiform, contingent, ambivalent and I call her my sex. Even if I make choices I still like everything. I like myself and you, but the hole we share accuses us both. I'll call it autofiction; on its head it accuses the world.

2. ON HIGH SCHOOL

VISITING HOURS ARE OVER FOR THE BLOODBATH, PLEASE

3. ON BEING A WIFE

Q: Are you polymorphously perverse?
A: No, I am betrothed to the present.

Consider the wife. *Desperately Seeking Susan*: Rosanna Arquette, wed to a jacuzzi and skimming the personals, rearranges the opposite side of the bridge. Anybody can be Madonna, so everybody's a wife in Fort Lee. Even the tubs dull the senses into a staycation. Arquette wants to be a club kid too, and briefly succeeds—at the precinct, in a gutted loft. Get into the groove and rot there, oh comely bohèmes! You'll even like it.

You say wife like style or you say wife like rifled through someone else's stocks or you say wife like wages. Wearing only animal print and plump in the right places. Dear Kay. Suspicious, you delayed wifery. Now you wear it like a polymer mink. Anybody can be a wife in the country like everybody's a piece in town.

Q: Does everybody feel this way?
A: I suspect they do, the fuckers

4. ON JOIE DE VIVRE

It comes out of me like *ohhhhhhhh*

5. ON BEAUTY

"By origin or not I am 'of' the city until I can't be—a choice, as choices go, made within constraints, one of which is surely beauty." I'm saying beauty like a person, not aesthetics like a grad student, though for my sins I'm the persona of a grad student and I've been one for long enough it feels like a condition.

You say aesthetics like style or you say aesthetics like a pretty face or you say aesthetics like a brand.

An aesthete says you can't write poems about sex if the city's full of brands. Or: art has no vocation after 1991. Or: beauty is a fixing for the wealthy, a commons in a paywall. Do I like this world and what it's full of? Like hell but there it goes, spitting you in the face and waiting for you underwater. You don't refuse to breathe, do you?

Meanwhile behind this handwringing the hushed suggestion that women, gays, transsexuals are especially to blame for the miseries of brands, or what the metropole inflicts on everybody else. Hello, I hate it. Or: how interesting, the smack of the feminized in buying and selling.

Dear Kay, hi, I'm waging a sub-rosa war. Who loves me will know what I mean.

6. ON GRIEF

It comes out of me like god fucking damnit......

7. ON LIES

Desire is the *suture* of a *new* (say it) world—*I'll fuck you till your dick is blue*—following Jackie's lead it won't be one of winners in a virtuous game, or letting agency skid off your ethical shoulders, or of sharing your toys based on a common Rx.

What are you and what does it mean for me a question nobody could stop asking if they wanted. *Re: perversion* you meant to say and follow it with something about *bodying forth the new* but Rachel heard one word played together like a chord. Say it's the same old sex bent double. It's mine now, and goes between me like a stent.

Dear Kay. I'm writing the same letter always, let me try it again. Here's a fable in the perfect tense: some friends—perpetually adolescent and vengeful, with a weekend off and no particular reputation—make the drive to bully a semi-famous writer. He's speaking at a private college for a couple hundred bucks a pop, the subject "modernist difficulty" or you get the idea. They've got a megaphone, which they use to frighten local wildlife. The poets they intended to swirlie have all fucked off to satisfy their appetites on bowls of seasonal produce. Or maybe the Rimbaldian creatures have their promised encounter after all, irritate the Tenure out of every mom and dad. Campus cops usher them off the handsome private greens. Over fries the *maudit* kids hum some poems about difficulty, poetry and rent, which makes them feel a little better—even triumphant!

Two of them are dating, and sort of clocky. En route back to a dingy apartment in the 'burbs some guy on the train resents the way their faces look, how they touch each other. He's got a couple slurs to share—his parting shot to "stay away from that AIDS." Which missile, however graphic, lets something slip.

I'd like to say that he got his but actually he got off at Newark without consequences. It's a shame for words to be more vibrant than sex—and sexier, too, says my enthusiastic boyfriend. Write back with something genuinely new, I won't be disconsolate or have anything unkind to say, palpating that world in a caress, your palpatrix on call,

Turner

SHUT YOUR MOUTH

Turner, hands
in a cookie jar. *How old
are you?* his trick asks. Turner counts backwards.
Shut your mouth. He drives,
oh, right into summer.

I COULD GO ON

Dear Jo—

Good morning, I'm shallow, sleepless, irrepressible. Does that endear me to you? 5 AM in March, wind smacks the skylight and hustles refuse over Flatbush like somebody's idea of a Zeitgeist. *Hi* it says *time to nap* but instead I'm writing testaments of what and who I love—Mike is sleeping in my bed warm and furred like a cat with a beard and a tattoo sleeve, maybe he would resent that description, I can do no other, I'm awake in another room achieving nothing in the second person singular, hello.

I do it for God and the television, with a promiscuous heart. I do it with prosthetics but apropos of anybody with an opinion about them: you are *forbidden* I want to say from evaluating my *component parts*, I'm an atom, fuck a metonymy, fuck a catalogue. First I composed that sentence, then I felt myself get eyebanged by every guy with a beard on the subway platform, don't think, Jo, I didn't sometimes return the favor. Mike's gone now, who brought me Oreos and spooned while I dreamt my nipples turned into mice and died, it's spring and I've been eyeing every aging wonder boy in the park plus his leanly pumping quads, their sprigs of magnificent hair, there's even crocuses, furious purple delicate violet contemptuous yellow, now I'm on a train, hello.

My imaginative lusts riddle bullet holes in the side of *the achievable*. Have you ever wanted to get fucked by an abdomen, an armpit, a couple of peddling legs? My preferred position with Cam for instance letting him piledrive my face from above, I lie down on my bed like a failed porn actor, I can imagine the camera fixed on my dewy lined eyes the bottom half of my face obscured under a cock and a tremendous Cupid's bow my cheeks sharp enough to be an architectural instrument as both of us try to remember our lines—but from this POV it's more like sex with a wiry frame and faded punk tattoos. Halfway into Jersey anyways and I'm thinking about your letter, poem, whatever, "All I Want by Joni Mitchell," where every paragraph begins *I want. I* is the letter's only person, *want* its only verb. It's Monday morning, what do I want? The flourishing of bees and grasses, never for anyone to pay rent, for the landlord to stop, for fuck's sake, *spying* on us, also a backyard, "it all . . . the whole world," to speak veritably about no appetite, never again authenticated, no more bad-faith prurience, my done taxes, a living wage for CUNY adjuncts, no moving apartments no falling to pieces, various men, if only they could finger, only some items impossible some are consequential, I fill up the tank and say goodnight and go, I could go on.

Patty Schemel writes in her memoir she joined Hole after "Doll Parts" was already cut but wrote a new drum line for the end and can still hear the more ambitious resonance of her snare in the final 16 bars or so sounding a hollow trench for Courtney's appetite   *I fake it so real*   I regularly dream I'm in a band but of course can play no instrument instead I writhe on stage exacerbating attention my face flushing well really my ears and my own desperate hot need to be seen, dear Jo, you get me.

So what if I want to be embarrassed? Usually I feel like telling anybody your dreams feels like showing your ass to strangers, well, so what if they look at what's good for them. Last night dreamt of being flat, ran all night to the top of my own dimension, night before the dream about the mice, then I came into possession of an immense stash, pursued by dream police I hid my ketamine in the pastel candy shop of other pharmaceuticals—even in dreams I can purloin a letter!—but the cops in my head got wise to the trick, even to a daring cinematic escape down a garbage chute where a "man with facial hair tries to recall my identity." By train through Jersey no spring here yet everything brown enclosed backyarded, and what have they done with my full stops, the Wawa in reach, I'm Dunkin, I'm somebody's sugary kid.

Call embarrassment less a discomfiting bug and more an intransigent object of megafixation, a hot flash an indisputable even if unconfirmed certainty of *occupying somebody's attention despite themselves* whether in vexation mockery or aimless arousal though maybe now my sense of shame a fruit rotted on the vine   like for instance to trick myself back to sleep watch videos of anybody else eating things I can't or won't like soups and noodles, foods on a stick, McDonalds breakfasts, lunch meats, eggs fried into toast oh hell   as in a *letter from* or *season in*   a staycation in hell   Good hell morning I haven't slept again I think I'm amorous infrastructure

Jo I think you're a lyricist of infatuation and I'm a geographer of arousal. What, if any, is the relevant difference, how will we be graded, I'm a slice of cake and cream, I'm Michelle Trachtenberg in *Mysterious Skin* and you're my malfortunate Joseph Gordon-Levitt, we applaud each others' poor decisions, late for work again goodnight you run up my phone bill I lie for hours in the hot water we toast with our remaining vices and make up about it, mutual spectators in the tragedy of semi-notorious men. Does that endear me to you? We're on the run from one to another parking lot, one of us a cavalier drifter with life by the balls, the other a neurotic but the better driver, with hair "the color of eyeliner" which am I? You're a caramelized peach, poached, juiced, even at a distance so inconvenient it'd take a day to reach you by bus on several tumescent roads.

Can you hear me where you sleep? Dear Jo. I want to finger-fuck my boyfriend in this bar, and I want you to know I'm thinking about it. Surprise!

With love at a boil,
Turner

"THE OPPOSITE"

Dear Kay:

What's the opposite of an anal fantasy

     a surname, a port of entry, Canada, 1993?

          When's the next Olympics? Am I a champion?

Unquestionable as a civic water supply

     Enthusiasm is the opposite of catastrophe

        Kyle MacLachlan is the opposite of Kyle MacLachlan

New Jersey is the opposite of New Jersey and New York, too

     for everybody without limits is the opposite of poptimism

Desire is the suture of a new (say it) world

     Coyness is the opposite of dissimulation not of
       something to say

        a glance in the right direction is the opposite of
          shut up and drive

Men buy me things is the opposite of waste

     writing you letters is the opposite of discretion

the opposite too of rotting gayly on anybody's own

coffee is the opposite of frenemies

extremely good as hell is the opposite of bohemian volume

villainy is not the opposite of a good time

Carly Rae is not the opposite of a good time

even the bourgeois O'Hara is not the opposite of a
good time

Rosario is not the opposite of a good time

Stephen is not the opposite of a good time

nor are you, Kay, the opposite of invective

you shouldn't even try to be the opposite of invective

responsive Niel is not the opposite of a good time

men in wool jackets are not the opposite of a good time

nor are *peintures idiotes* but they come pretty close

a capable tonguefuck not the opposite of a good time

obliging dads are not the opposite of a good time

no more than their obliging wallets

Neither Liam nor William Morris the opposite of a good time

Jo is not the opposite of a good time

Rimbaud the gay romanticism is probably the opposite
of a good time

just as Rimbaud the commune invective is not

it's Rimbaud v. Rimbaud in the Port Authority MECHA crunch!

teaching is not the opposite of a good time but shit pay is

saying something new is not the opposite of a good time

a truly singular stache is not the opposite of a good time

Connie is not the opposite of a good time

exuberant Andreas are not the opposite of a good time

Menergy ft. Sylvester is not the opposite of a good time

Nick Cage in *Moonstruck* is not the opposite of a good time

Jackie the recluse not the opposite of a good time

objectivist hamburgers not the opposite of a good time

no more than the dog who refuses them for traffic

no more than handsome consciousness

no more than staunch persuasion

no more than Takis, substitution

no more than delts like hubcaps

no more than taut personas

no more than appetizing musks

no more than a boyfriend surplus

no more than tasteless amateurs

no more than wind tunnel belligerence

no more than accommodating tissue

no more than inappropriate sizing

no more than slovenly comportment

no more than intimate addressees

no more than minor personality

no more than an impressive paunch

no more than months of back pay (credit)

no more than land and water

no more than sleepless want

no more than the plenitude of the 90s

no more than the thigh under the buttock

no more than structuring fixations

(I have structuring fixations)

no more than nipples, boys, beer, Dunkin

no more than dolls to wake and sleep to

If I am buoyed or cowed by the social I am still in it, a queen in Bucks
County

naked, oppositional, emphatic, love,

Turner, red and spitting

NOTES

A partial list: this book collages language, character and image from Viktor Shklovsky's *Zoo, or Letters Not About Love*, Jacqueline Susann's *Valley of the Dolls*, the film *Cruising*, the gay pornographic periodical *Straight to Hell*, and Marx's *Capital*, Vol. 3. The polemic in "Travel Advisory for Constance Augusta" is informed by my reading of, in particular, Viviane Namaste's *Invisible Lives* and Emma Heaney's *The New Woman*. The title *A Queen in Bucks County* is lifted from canto 12 of Louis Zukofsky's "A".

ACKNOWLEDGMENTS

Excerpts from A Queen in Bucks County appeared in the following publications: "Peripheral XO" in *Salvage Quarterly*, "Shut Your Mouth" in *Mirage/Periodical*, "You Say Wife" in *Social Text*, "I Could Go On" in The Poetry Project's *The Recluse*. My thanks to the editors: Jordy Rosenberg, Dodie Bellamy and Kevin Killian, Marie Buck and the staff at the Project.

Heartfelt thanks to Diana Hamilton and Jameson Fitzpatrick, who offered careful suggestions on some of the letters during their fall 2019 workshop for The Poetry Project on poetry in sentences, and to Shiv Kotecha, who invited me to read from the manuscript at his Château reading series, also in 2019. Rachel Levitsky read several drafts of the book during our Emerge-Surface-Be Fellowship together, and helped guide it along to its final version. Amy De'Ath, Jordy Rosenberg, and McKenzie Wark approached this project with the kind of criticism and integrity that made it possible for me to take it seriously.

To Constance Augusta Zaber, Jo Barchi, Niel Rosenthalis and Stephen Ira: thanks for the permissiveness, for being written to, and for writing back.

My love and thanks to Aaina Amin, Addison Vawters, Adelita Husni-Bey, Becca Teich, Ben Mabie, Chris Berntsen, Emily Lim Rogers, Hannah Black, Harron Walker, Jackie Ess, Liam O'Brien, Marie Buck, Max Fox, Mike Funk, Patrick DeDauw, Rosario Inés, Ry Dunn, Rylee Lyman, Tracy Rosenthal and Trish Salah—for being there, and for talking about it.

Thanks to everyone at Nightboat for approaching this book with enormous care: Caelan Ernest Nardone, Gia Gonzales, Lina Bergamini, Lindsey Boldt, Stephen Motika. Thanks to Kit Schluter for the design.

To Cam Scott: you gave this book tremendous attention, and you liked it better the weirder it got. These letters are not not about love. Thanks. You're welcome.

KAY GABRIEL is a poet, essayist and teacher. She's the author of *Kissing Other People or the House of Fame* (Rosa Press, 2021) and *Elegy Department Spring: Candy Sonnets 1* (BOAAT Press, 2017). With Stephen Ira and Liam O'Brien she coedited *Vetch*, a poetry magazine for trans writers, and with Andrea Abi-Karam she coedited *We Want It All: An Anthology of Radical Trans Poetics* (Nightboat, 2020). Kay is currently part of the editorial collective for the *Poetry Project Newsletter*. She lives in Queens.

NIGHTBOAT BOOKS

Nightboat Books, a nonprofit organization, seeks to develop audiences for writers whose work resists convention and transcends boundaries. We publish books rich with poignancy, intelligence, and risk. Please visit nightboat.org to learn about our titles and how you can support our future publications.

The following individuals have supported the publication of this book. We thank them for their generosity and commitment to the mission of Nightboat Books:

Kazim Ali
Anonymous (4)
Abraham Avnisan
Jean C. Ballantyne
The Robert C. Brooks Revocable Trust
Amanda Greenberger
Rachel Lithgow
Anne Marie Macari
Elizabeth Madans
Elizabeth Motika
Thomas Shardlow
Benjamin Taylor
Jerrie Whitfield & Richard Motika

This book is made possible, in part, by grants from the New York City Department of Cultural Affairs in partnership with the City Council and the New York State Council on the Arts Literature Program.